LOTUS &

THE

APOCALYPSE

AUSTIN DAVIS

Outcast Press

Fiction From the Fringes

www.Outcast-Press.com

(print) ISBN-13: 978-1-7379829-3-7
(e-book) ASIN: B09QLZMHT3

Grateful acknowledgement is made to Myla K. Smart from the Etsy shop @ArtnNeedles for providing phenomenal artwork, as well the editors of the following publications where some of these poems first appeared:

✳✳✳

Button Poetry, Emerge Literary Journal, Ghost City Press, Maudlin House, Okay Donkey Magazine, and *The Tempe Writers Forum*

TABLE OF CONTENTS

The World Will End Tonight – Pg. 7

THE WORLD WILL END TONIGHT

the weatherman says,
when the flower heads twist down
at a quarter past six.

Remember that summer of hot breath,
open windows, and making love
to the sound of bicycles passing by?

Kiss me soft
as the clouds peel away
from the sun like dark yellow apple skins.

Let me hold you,
run my hands through your hair,
these last few minutes.

LOTUS & FEAR

there's a yellow balloon, the color of autumn after snow,
bouncing around my chest

i often mistake its rhythm for my heartbeat,
so trust me,
i know i can't be trusted

let's play a party game
where we have to take turns telling each other
about all of our fears and mistakes
and take a shot each time we wish we had a time machine

we'll be blackout drunk
before the guests start ringing our doorbell

last night i broke into my old elementary school
and left a coffee mug full of wet dirt and seeds
in the janitor's closet
to see if it's possible for a flower to grow tall and bright
under the glow of a lightbulb on a string

i've always thought of happiness as being tangible
the most brilliant mango hanging from the highest branch

but if we can't even find the forest,
how are we supposed to climb the tree?

each day numbs me into dismissiveness
until my lips are purple from wine

and i'm sitting on the patio

watching the rain darken the red brick tiles around my feet

fill my lungs with hot breath
and we'll blow out the candles together

sing that familiar tune
learn how to pop without a sound

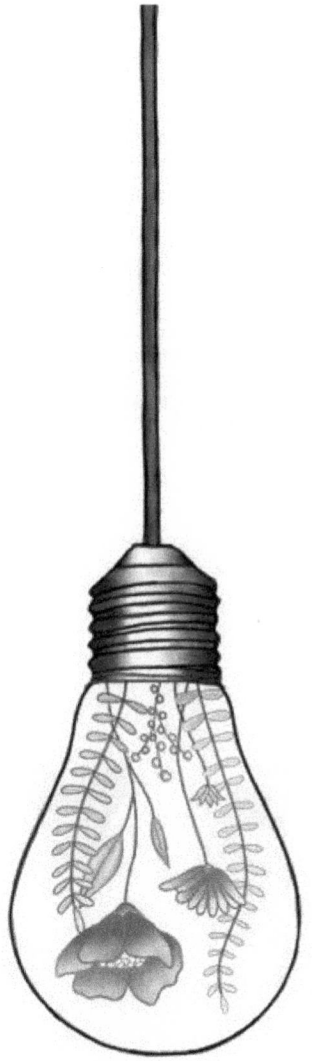

Artwork by Myla K. Smart

LOTUS & LOVE

We meet up in the library parking lot
every night after you get off work
at the drugstore.

We lie on the roof of my van
and stare up at the sky.
You call the stars "cosmic freckles"
and tell me that our biology teacher
from high school buys glow-in-the-dark

condoms and that the "v"
on the middle of a Valium pill
looks like a little heart
that wants more than anything
to become a circle.

I nod and laugh and think
about how we're both going to die
some night in our sleep
and we'll never see it coming.

The leaves have no idea they're going to fall,
the fish have no idea they're going to be eaten
by an unhappy family around a big oak table,

and you have no idea
that getting to hear about your day
for 32 and a half minutes
every night is what makes me okay
with waking up in the morning.

I suppose this is the way living has always been.
You think you're happy until you meet that person
who makes you notice every ache in your chest.

Maybe we should drive my van
into the book deposit bin
and steal all the books
our consciences can carry.

Maybe we should make out
or make love or make up
some story about a little home
in the mountains

with art on the walls,
a pineapple pizza
cooking in the oven, and "1979"
by The Smashing Pumpkins
playing on a ham radio in the kitchen.

In my mind you're pulling into the driveway
in the same car you're driving tonight,
about to lie with me by the fireplace

on our rug of pink and yellow orchids,
tell me all about the last 10 hours

of your existence,

and make me feel like
the man who cried into the clouds
during a solar eclipse

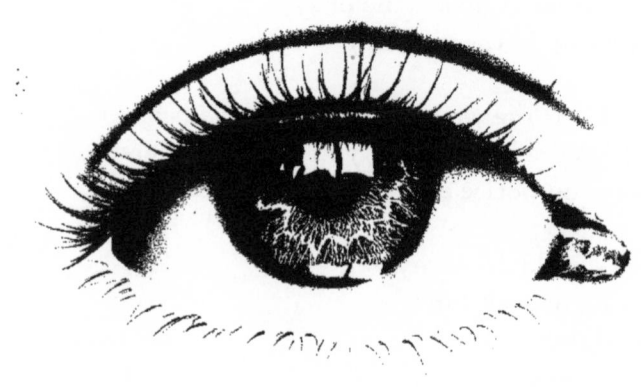

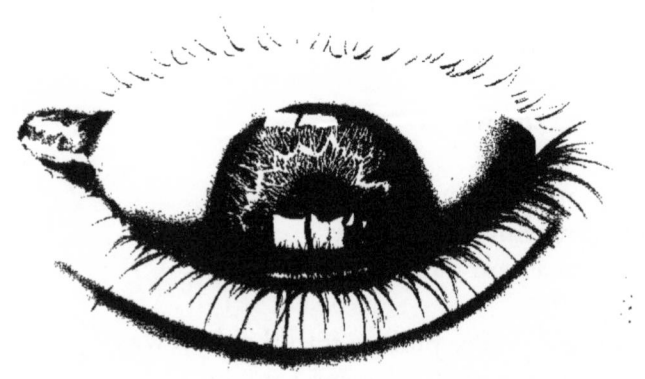

LOTUS & SUMMER

i'm sitting in the driveway
at 6:24 pm

running my hands through black gravel
and Arizona flower bits

i'm sad

i need comfort
but my face feels like an ice cream cone
dripping onto a tongue of wind

the world is thick and slow

god is churning us in his hands like wet clay
hoping his universe will resemble something
of a vase after it leaves the kiln

a hearty soup or an electric blanket
might just kill me
darling

so please,
when i walk through the door tonight,
pull me to the kitchen floor
before i can think or cry or worse

bite my lip as our toes trace the cracks
in the tile around the refrigerator

lick my neck and lie about the weather

LOTUS & SEX

The image of you tonight stepping out of the shower
with a towel around your hair

will be the screensaver in my brain
until the day they cut me open for science.

I'm halfway out the window, lighting a cigarette.

You smile at me from the doorway
and finger a mountain range with a wavy stream,
puffy clouds, and a grinning sun

on the steamed up mirror as if you're hoping
that if you just keep drawing, it'll thicken into a window.

Your footprints on the bathroom floor
look like little turtles crawling back to the ocean

and in this moment, I want to fall
from our apartment on the fifth story a little less.

Let's make love on the wet tile,
tonguing up and down each other's bodies

until we both believe that the sun will never rise or set.

I had a dream that daybreak is just a camera flash
and the color of our day prints across the sky
all inky and soft in the evening.

I don't know the difference between what is real

and what I'm most afraid of,

but you've blown out the candle on our bedside table
and are crawling into bed, smelling like coconut soap
and the promise of a warm tomorrow,

so I know I can smile for the photographer,
even if he is God.

LOTUS &

DEPRESSION

I.

last night
as I was driving to your apartment

i threw up
whatever the hell was in my stomach
all over the steering wheel
and hit a feral cat

i named her Pythagoras
and dug her a grave
with my car keys

next to a patch of purple
wildflowers by the highway

it scared me that I drove away and didn't cry

II.

what's the difference
between a handful of benzos

and you holding my face in your hands
and assuring me i'll be okay?

do you ever feel like
an amoeba in a drop of water on mars

when i'm struggling to keep my eyes open
and you notice how much weight i've lost?

III.

i keep thinking i'll step out
of this rough patch eventually,

but the grass has grown so high,
i can feel it brush along my lips

you don't like how bony my shoulders are
but we still touch each other sometimes

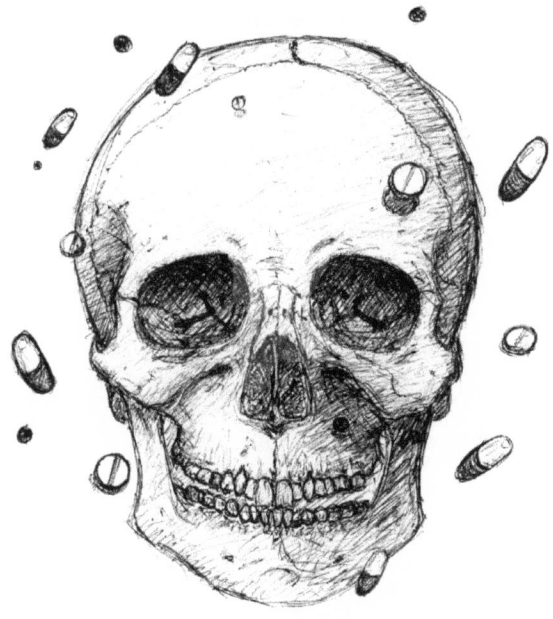

LOTUS & ANOTHER DAY

At the grocery store
the cashier doesn't ask how my day is going.

He stares behind me
out the long glass window
and bags my beer.

I don't ask how he's doing either.

This morning my little sister brought
a photo of our family at the beach
to her class for show and tell.

Dad is mid-sneeze.
My sister is shaking sand from her hair.

My brother and I stand on our tiptoes,
fighting over who's taller.

Mom smiles.

In class the kids
pass the pictures
around in a circle,

holding them close
to their little faces,

smudging us with their fingers.

I'm sorry I keep changing the subject.

The sky is falling
more and more
each day

and I'm afraid of what will happen
when I reach
to touch the clouds

and only grab air.

LOTUS & OBLIVION

on the bad days
my heart
is a pile of shit
rotting away my ribs

i know that's a gross metaphor
but i've heard
that art is for honesty

and honestly
i haven't showered
or left my bed
in days

my eyes are heavy
from the pills

i'm nodding off,
picturing Jesus
heating up a bowl
or flicking a needle

      remember when we
      stole that bottle of Jack
      and those red solo cups
      from Walmart

      rode our bikes
      up the bridge
      over the 202

and jammed each cup
in to the chain-link fence
in the shape
of a middle finger?

the cars below us
kept honking

and our "fuck you"
kinda looked like
an uncircumcised penis

and when i told you that,
you laughed so hard
you spit whiskey at me

God uses scare tactics
so we don't notice the devil

but let me tell you, baby

purgatory is far
worse than Hell

this night
feels like the silence
after a record ends

i blow smoke to the ceiling
as the music drops from the air

the needle stays bouncing
like a rowboat over black waves
and i think about what my doctor said
in a dream last night

we were at a Rangers' game
and he was a talking javelina,
drinking Bud Light
but he told me

"to get well,
you have to wring out your brain
like a dirty sponge
and let the dark rain pool around your feet"

i reach for the razor
on our bedside table
and comb my hair down the middle

like an '80s heartthrob
who just got divorced
and needs to feel young for a moment

soon there's blood on our bed sheets
soon my hands are twisting and twisting
soon our apartment is flooded with ink

LOTUS & HONESTY

Lotus lives in a 1 bedroom flat
above a laundromat.
He listens to the washing machines
spin and turn all night like ocean waves.

Lotus either sleeps all day or not at all
and he'll do anything not to think.

He watches reruns of old sitcoms
and basketball games from the '90s
under a weighted blanket and smokes a blunt in bed
even though his sheets get sticky with ash.

Lotus hurts like the moon would hurt
if it was in love with the sun.

His friends don't know what drugs he uses,
or that he often thinks about dying.

Logan and Will would say he's just a heavyweight,
that he likes to go hard on Friday nights
and have a good time.

Logan and Will have steady jobs
and girlfriends who get along.

They work all week and double date every other Saturday.

They talk about marriage and babies
and buying little brick houses in the suburbs
within walking distance of top-rated schools.

Will doesn't get anxious around big groups of people
and Logan has never cut his thigh with a razor blade.

Lotus tries to be a good person
but some nights he's not.

Some nights he closes his eyes
and floors it down a dark strip of highway
in the early morning.

It's dreamy and sad
to fly through the night
with your heart pounding in your throat,
ears ringing like church bells,

vision swimming under salt water.

Lotus is terrified of rear-ending
an old lady with insomnia,
terrified of all the bad thoughts in his head,

terrified about what could happen
before the sun rises.

It's like becoming a balloon
that's blown up
with helium instead of breath,

a balloon that's let go of,

a balloon that flies towards the stars
until it pops.

INTERLUDE

there once was a plastic rocket

that two kids rode to space

the destination was forever

but the boy stared into the sun

and burned away his face

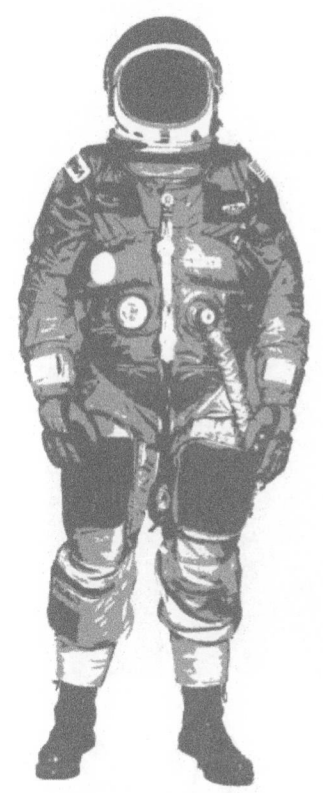

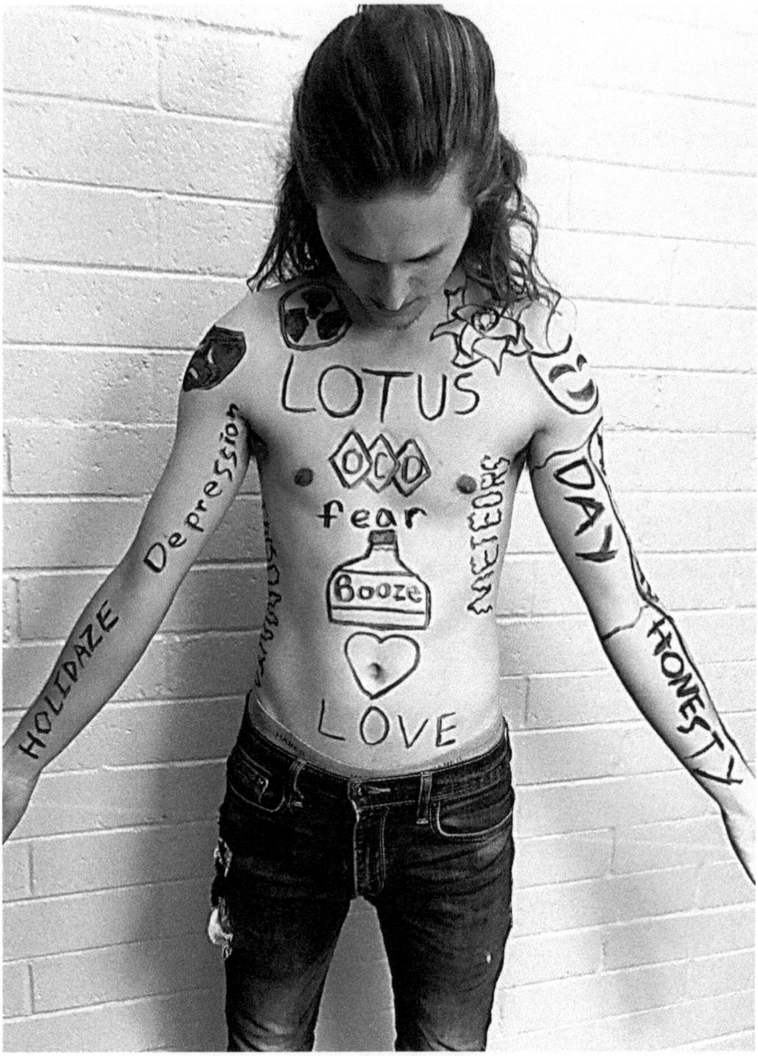
LOTUS
OCD
fear
Booze
LOVE
Depression
HOLIDAZE
METEORS
DAY
HONESTY

LOTUS & THE METEORS

I.

meteors
are
falling

but
i don't think
meteors

are
really
falling

II.

fish swim
through
the sky

white bones,
licked clean,
drop slow

like clouds
that've seen
some real shit

& have
hardened
over time

III.

our home
has vanished
from the neighborhood

all that's left
is a brick patio
with lawn chairs

a few
cigarette butts
beside ashes

IV.

there's probably
a little moss
green house

with teddy bear drapes
pulled across the windows
posted up on Mars

the tv is still on
the dog is peeing
all over the carpet

& i'm sorry baby
but i left the stove on
on purpose

LOTUS & BOOZE

I got so fucked up last night,
I walked home from Casey's
and passed out on our front porch.

I woke up with my head
on the welcome mat,

our neighbor's cat
sniffing my hair
as if I was a dead bird.

The sun had barely risen
and you were still asleep.

I imagined that maybe
when you went to bed last night,
you brushed your teeth,
washed your face,
and thought to yourself that maybe
I hadn't come home yet

because I was fighting some fire
and saving a family of orphans
who were trapped under a piano.

Or, maybe you thought
I was at the mall,
picking out diamond earrings for you
right at closing time,

when a man in a black ski mask

kicked the glass doors open
and pointed a gun
at the cashier.

The cashier couldn't be much older
than we were the first night we kissed,
and she looked just as frightened
as I felt when you said
you'd always love me,
but didn't look me in the eyes.

Hell to that, in this fantasy, I didn't think
about you. No. Too much
was at stake.

The cashier
held her hands up high
and gasped as I ducked behind
a case of gleaming watches.

The man waved his pistol
like a baton
at the end of a relay.
All I could see were his eyes,
but in the morning

I'll tell you how scared he was, darling,
how frightened he was
of life and death,
of failure and guilt.

He never saw it coming
when I tackled him to the ground
and bashed his face
into the coat rack.

I'd tell you all this,
but none of it is true.
I just got sad again last night
and threw away another paycheck.

You know this,
and I know that's why
you didn't call last night.

I poke my head in the doorway
of our bedroom.
You're wearing my Cookie Monster
T-shirt, the one that looks like
a dress on you,
and I think about smiling,
but I don't.

I just walk barefoot to the bathroom
and throw up a bit in my mouth.

I floss between each tooth,
spit blood and watch it wash away
in the sink. I think to myself,

One healthy habit is better than none.

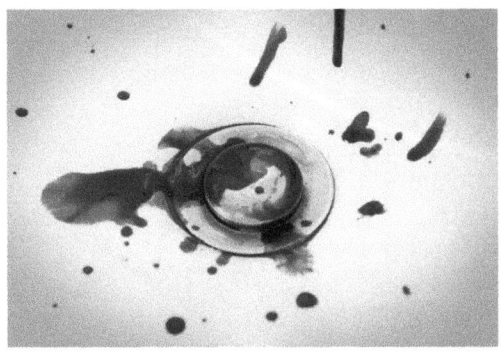

LOTUS & ...

if it was always night

the crickets
outside our window

would be gluttonous
& addicted to sex

but i don't give a fuck

you'd still be
in bed

breathing out your nose
on my neck

morning would never come

we wouldn't have to talk
about the flames
inching up our lawn

or how they're brighter
than any sunrise
we've ever seen

LOTUS &

HALLUCINATIONS

You used to call me
at my home
on your purple rotary phone
with the really long extension cord
every evening when the sky
turned its darkest black.

This was during a time
when everything was funny
but no one knew how to laugh.

All the living rooms in every city
were filled with mothers watching
their game shows,
spooning peas and custard
into their mouths
from the microwaves on their laps.

All the garages in every suburb
were filled with weeping fathers,
balancing on their heads
like clowns after sex
who had run out of cigarettes.

We used to watch the fathers
from doorway to doorway
as they hit something with a hammer

that didn't need to be fixed.

I kept my phone duct taped to my chest
all day, waiting for your call,
but when the phone did ring,
all sad and quiet,

I waited twelve and a half seconds
before answering. I knew it was you.
You knew it was me.
But who wants to admit that to themselves?

I'd pick up the phone
and you'd be chewing gum on the other end,
like always, and you'd blow
another pink bubble out of your mouth,
hoping it would float you to me.
It never did.

As I spit a ball of snot on to the shadows
dancing along my wall, you would say,
from your throat, not your teeth,

Not everything needs to be fixed, Lotus.
Some houses are built with the wrong bricks.
Don't blame the painter
for trying to color a hole, Lotus.
Did you know that your skin
crawls at night when you're alone in bed
because there are ALWAYS ladybugs making love
underneath your toenails?

It's a shame your eyes
are on the opposite end of your body,
isn't it, Lotus? Haven't you ever blinked
yourself to life in complete darkness

and screamed and screamed
until the walls closed in around you,
trying to get you to shut the hell up?

Haven't you ever awoken to sunshine
and cried and cried so long,
your bed sunk deep into the earth
thinking maybe you'd sprout one day like a dandelion
if you knew what the dirt tasted like?

Some seeds won't turn into grass, Lotus.
Some seeds will feed the birds.
Some seeds will kill the squirrels.
Some seeds will explode
in your motherfucking stomach.

Across the hall,
in every cradle in every upstairs,
there was a baby
wishing someone would hug him.
He didn't know what a hug was,
and he didn't know why he wanted one,
but he could feel his skin growing old.
He knew he hadn't been touched since he was a goldfish.

In every attic above every hell,
there was a girl kissing her elbows
over and over again, reassuring the birds
resting on the windowsill that
If a tattoo can be removed, so can a scar.

I used to walk from room to room
while you spoke to me,
looking in on the people I loved as they fell apart.

The world is a broken lightbulb

no one cares enough about to sweep up.
Please, Lotus,
lick the glass
until your tongue bleeds sunlight.

I mouthed along to your words
as you said them
as if they were a song
and not a suicide.

You could never see me
over the phone, but you could hear
the click of my lips
and the snap of my spit
matching yours,
and when you finally stopped talking,
we felt the bubble pop all over our faces.

In that silence,
we both knew
that for the rest of the night,
at least we'd still be in love.

LOTUS & INSOMNIA

i don't remember
the last time i slept through the night

i'm so exhausted
my bones feel like soldiers
who shot themselves in war
& were sent home
to their families

when it's late i walk & do drugs
& end up somewhere new

tonight i'm at a park
in a sleepy neighborhood
& i miss my mom
& i hate myself
i puke all over a dead bush

i could wipe it up
with the greasy mcdonald's napkins
in my back pocket
but i don't

the sky is clear,
the moon a purple brown

i'm not sure what that means
but if i've learned 1 thing in this life

anything can feel like a metaphor
if you're scared enough

LOTUS & THE

HOLIDAZE

5 ft under
ground

the weather
is 3 months
behind

i'm celebrating Halloween

while my love,
my parents,
my friends from high school,

the whole world above me
welcomes in the new year

i spit until i make mud

sculpting masks in my hands
and trying on different faces

tonight I'm a vampire
with sticky soil
between my teeth

later I'll be the devil

or maybe a rabbit
if my horns get too floppy

to be sane
is to find peace

to be alive

is to let go
the way a drunk
falls off a barstool

it happens quick
on accident
half asleep

when the ball drops
all glorious with light

you'll have your streamers
but i'll have the worms

LOTUS & THE CRASH

I.

i send the tire
from some guy's Jeep
spinning into
the freeway

glass rains
over my head
and burns like snow

i see my breath

he looks like Wes

the dick
from high school
who stole a pair of handcuffs
from his dad's police belt

and threw me into the dumpster
behind the cafeteria
like end-of-the-week meat
one night in summer

II.

tonight
Wes who isn't Wes

breaks my nose

like the airbag
should have

he wipes blood
from my face

and smears it on
my lips
like makeup

i see flowers

flowers
between his teeth

flowers
in the broken glass
sparkling up the freeway

flowers
in the flames

III.

the apocalypse is here

worms fly
from a fire hydrant

the tattoos on Wes' neck
peel off his skin
and launch at me

a tremor tears the city in half
and a blue station wagon

shoots off the bridge

no one seems to notice
the clouds falling
from the sky

IV.

covered in soot
i break into
my parents' house
through the window

i crawl into bed
between them

mom flips over on her side

a tree taps
at the window
and i think of how
my dad used to tell me

that during a bad storm
either the branch will break
or the wind will stop

and the wind will always stop
eventually

so the tree just has
to hold together
until morning

i look up at the fan
and imagine all the stars

and planets

the endless silence
on the other side
of the ceiling

i speak
a prayer

and someone says,
"bless you"
in their sleep

LOTUS & LOSS

I.

If you point your telescope up on this clear summer night,
you might be able to spot Lotus.

He's probably too small to see from your backyard,
but hey, you could tell your kids
that any one of those airplanes
could be him, falling back to Earth.

Right about now, Lotus is swimming through nothingness,
like he has been for longer than he knows.

Back in the rocket on Mars, Lotus' captain
is smoking his 4th cigarette
and banging his fist against the table over and over again.

The crew is shuffling away to the edge of the little kitchen
as their coffee mugs bounce up and down.

On Earth, mission control is in a code red.
Every telescope from NY to LA is focused on
finding their stick of hay in a pile of needles.

Unfortunately for NASA, a little college newspaper
caught word about Lotus.

Within an hour, every news station in the country
was talking about this poor boy from Prairie Creek
on their evening broadcast.

Every kid with a pair of binoculars
is straining out their window
right about now, scanning the sky until bedtime.

II.

When you're hurtling through space
slower than Mrs. Huckles
rides her electric scooter through the supermarket,
you have a lot to think about.

For a while, Lotus screamed. He screamed and screamed,
flailing about for God knows how long.

Lotus thought of his mother giving him a hug on
Thanksgiving, drinking beer with his friends on the roof,
the children and wife he never met.

Lotus cried. He cried so long,
the blackness began to look like a cape
he thought he might be able to grab in his hands
and pull away to unveil autumn in his little town,
where everything would be okay again.

Lotus thought about movie theaters,
wind chimes, school buses and making love.

He thought about being a kid and spending his summers
trying to touch the bottom of Wilson's lake
but never having enough breath.

He thought about biting into a peach, falling off a bike,
being so tired you pass out on the couch
with the TV still on,
and how bodies don't decompose in space.

Lotus will be 21 years, 4 months, and 18 days old
until the sun explodes.

He couldn't wipe his eyes in his space suit and helmet,
so the tears dried on his cheeks.

Maybe Lotus would be found
by a time travelling orangutan
or a teenage alien who ran away from their planet
in the angstiest possible way.

Or maybe he wouldn't be found.
Maybe that would be just as well.

Lotus closed his eyes and saw nothing
but the color of wind.

MORE FROM OUTCAST PRESS

International travels and ayahuasca, oh my! A novel about friendship dragged through the Amazon jungle and spit out through the stars with the aid of decades, DMT, and well-meaning debauchery. Now available on Amazon, Kindle, SmashWords, Barnes & Nobel, & more!

Available March, 2022

Henry Gallagher is going to die. His liver is failing and his chances of living past 30 crumble around him. He revels in a parade of violence, blackouts, half-hearted AA meetings, psych ward stints, dangerous sexual encounters, suicidal behavior, and shattered relationships.

During his darkest hour, he receives an offer that threatens to change his life forever and a mental diagnosis that, in Henry's mind, makes him more monster than man.

ABOUT THE AUTHOR

Twitter: @ Austin_Davis17   Instagram: @AustinWDavis1

Austin Davis doesn't know who the hell Lotus is. He got really high one night and wrote this book. Austin is a poet and activist, studying creative writing at ASU and leading Arizona Jews For Justice's unsheltered outreach program, AZ Hugs For the Houseless. Davis is also the author of *The World Isn't the Size of Our Neighborhood Anymore* (Weasel Press, 2020) and *Celestial Night Light* (Ghost City Press, 2020).

His new album of jazz-poetry about homelessness, in collaboration with Joe Allie, is called *Street Sorrows* out on all streaming services. Davis likes late nights at dive bars with people he'd die for, skateboarding down a hill after sunset with his eyes closed, and trying his best not to be too sad about the state of humanity. His website is www.Msha.ke/AustinDavis

CPSIA information can be obtained
at www.ICGtesting.com
Printed in the USA
LVHW031145230222
711788LV00004B/554